Special Thoughts
For
Special People

by Judith Ann Schwartz

Special Thoughts for Special People
Written and Illustrated by Judith Ann Schwartz
Angelee Coleman Grider, Editor

Printed in the United States of America
ISBN 978-0-9820354-9-8 (Revised Edition, Copyright © 2008)

M.O.R.E. Publishers Corp.
P.O. Box 38285
St. Louis, MO 63138
MOREPublishersCO@AOL.com

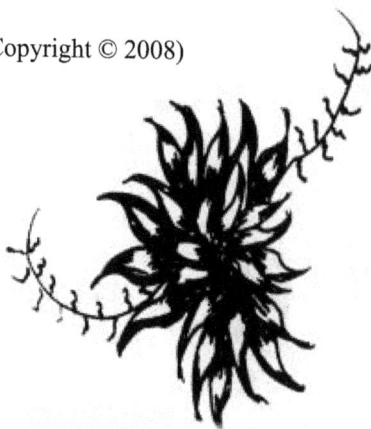

I wrote this book to share with
those who enjoy reading poetry.

Some may see God's power
shining through.

If anything I have written
has helped anyone in any way,
that is my reward.

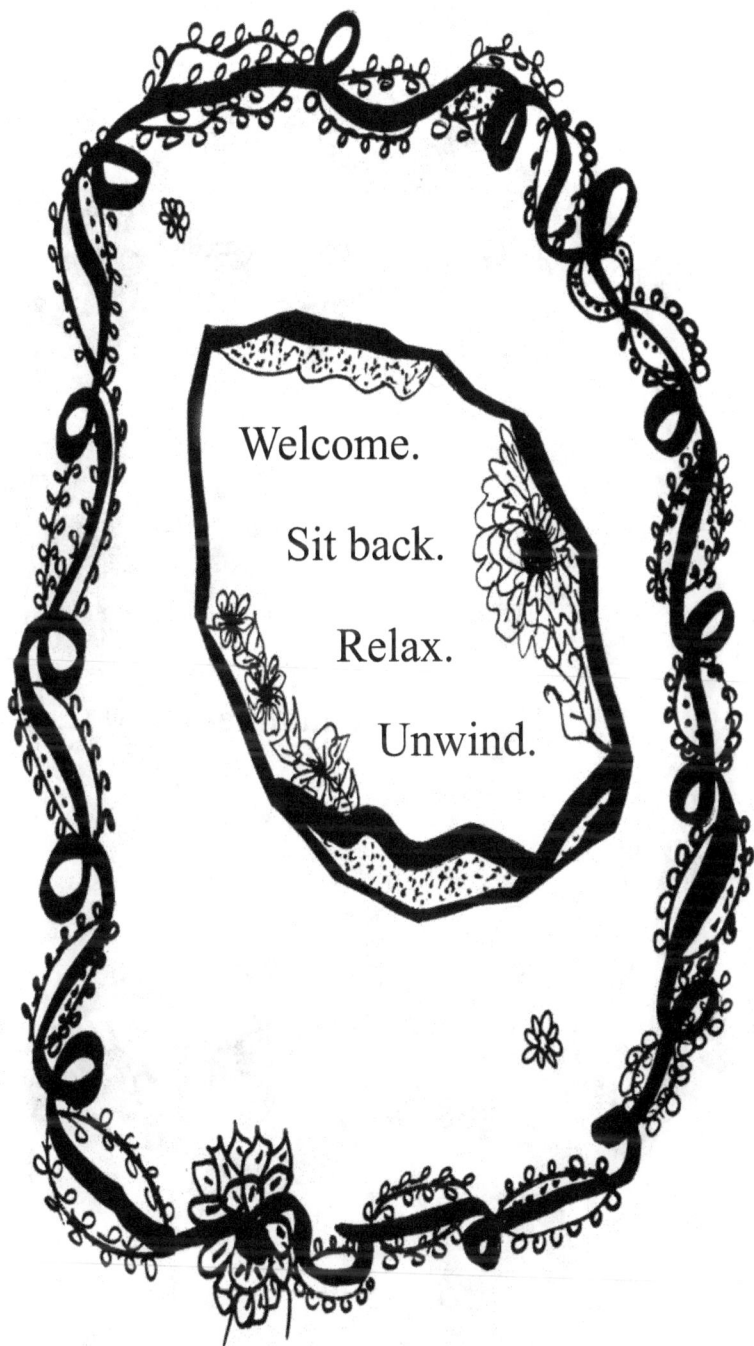

Welcome.

Sit back.

Relax.

Unwind.

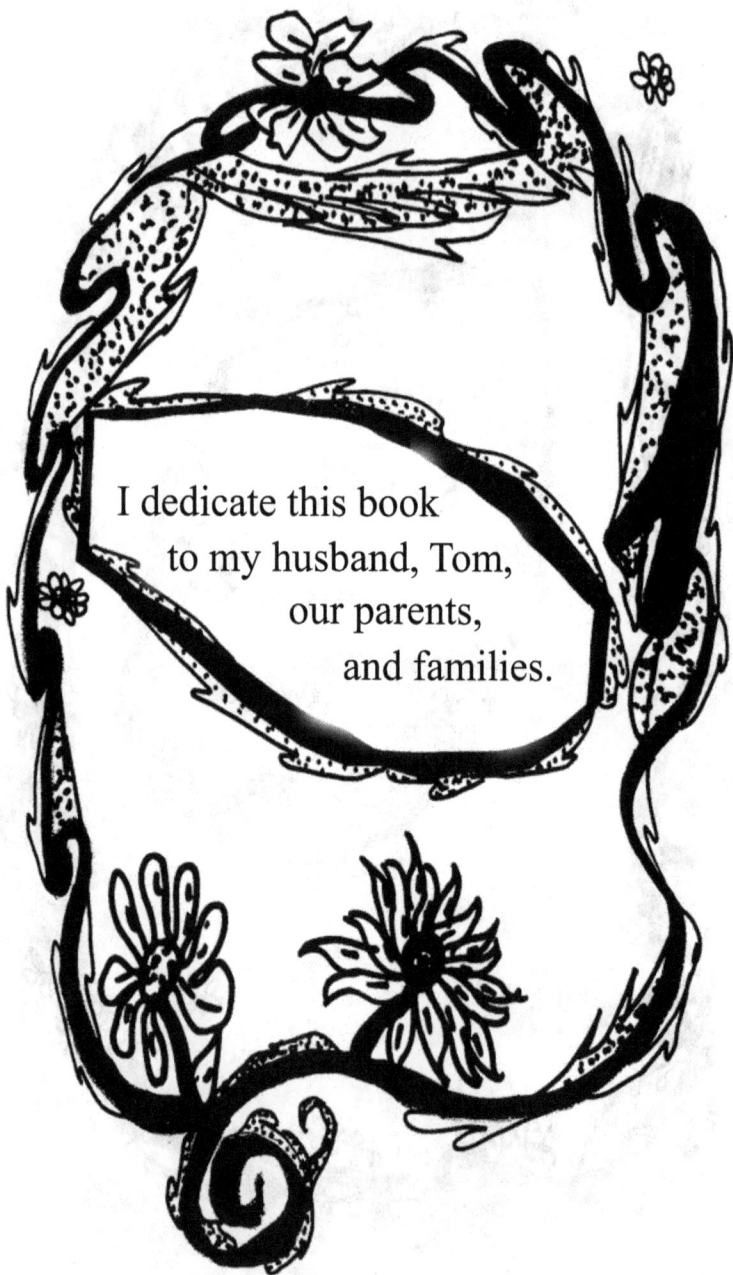

I dedicate this book
to my husband, Tom,
our parents,
and families.

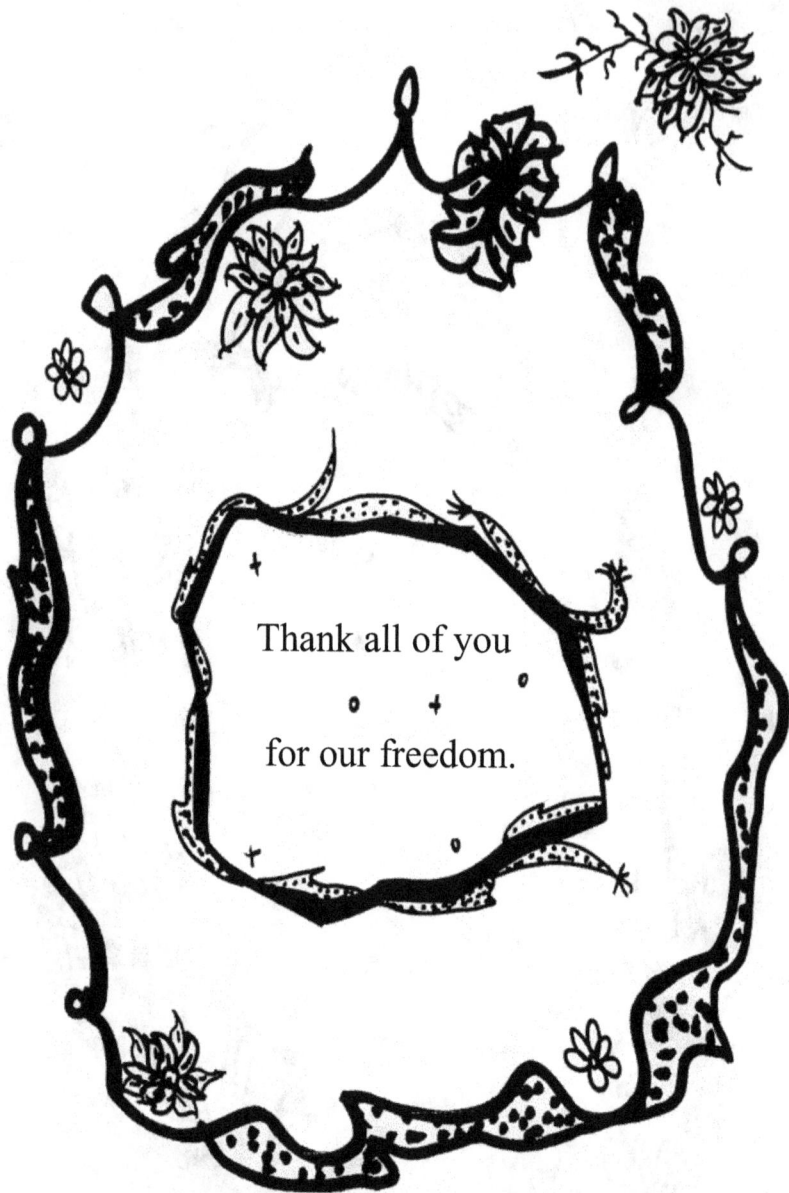

Thank all of you

for our freedom.

8

To all the military men and women,

Just want you to know,

That we appreciate

ALL OF YOU

THANKS

May God keep all of you safe,

and bring you home

the same way.

May their hearts be blessed

by the Lord forever.

In Our Thoughts Forever

As our days go by,

let's not forget 9/11,

all those families that lost

their loved ones,

and the sadness that followed.

Let's keep all those special people

in our prayers

for they will never forget

that awful day.

May God comfort them

now and always.

Flash Floods

Wildfires   Hurricanes

Katrina

Avalanches

Tornadoes

Volcanoes

NEED WE

SAY MORE

Please don't forget all those

who lost their homes and everything

they owned.

Never forget that dreadful day.

I do hope they are getting along in life.

I just want them to know that the world will

never forget the sadness.

We will keep you in our prayers.

Thanks to all the special helpers.

I'm sure the word "why" was said

a million times,

but no one will ever know why,

but God.

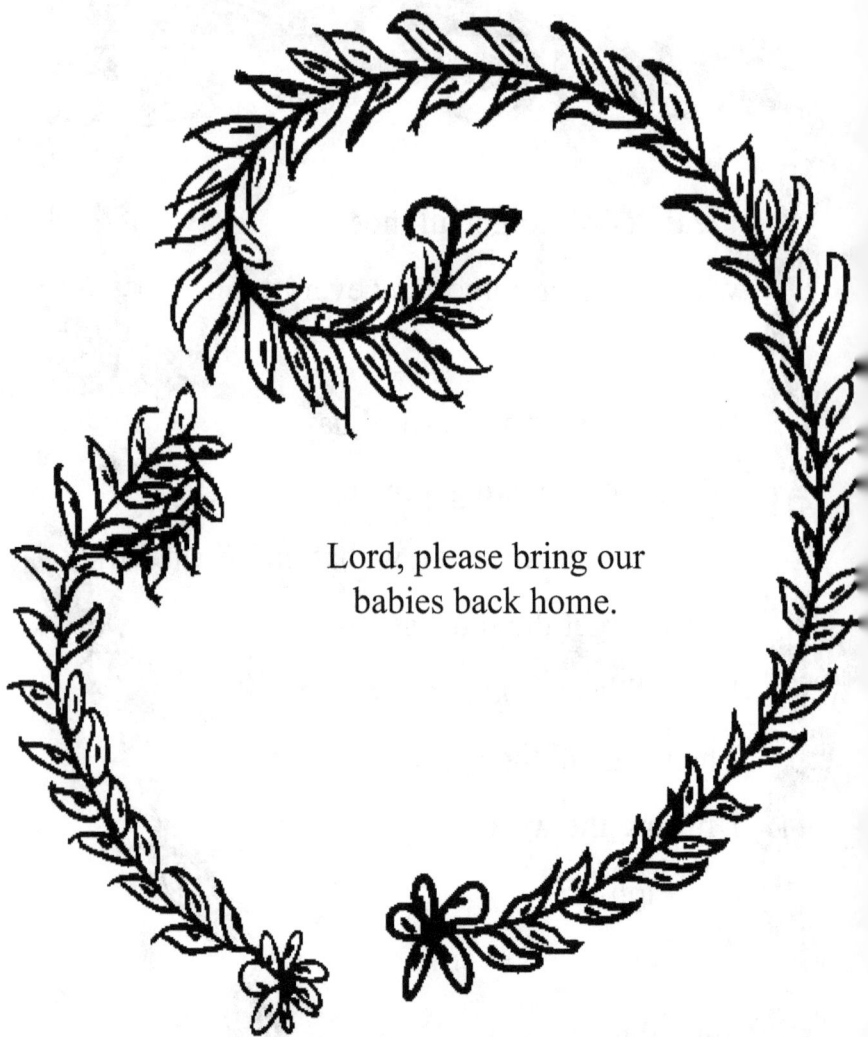

Lord, please bring our
babies back home.

Dearest Lord,

It's so very hard not knowing where all
these children have gone.

Please Lord, return these children to their
families and loved ones.

Lord, please comfort them,

and care for them,

for we love them so.

Love your Dad.
He is so special.
Treasure him until the end.

Lord, I don't want to be a bother,

just want to thank you for my

dear father.

His heart was full of love,

and he was always there for me.

He worked hard all his life, and cared

for his children and his wife.

Lord, he was a blessing

and he made a difference

in my life.

A Mother's love is forever –
from beginning to end.

If I could live this day over
What would I change
Or maybe rearrange?
Would I think of myself or maybe others?
No, I think I'd take time out and
Call my Mother.

Mothers are so special
Love and respect them until the end
And the memories will be yours
To keep.

A brother IS
a
gift from God.

A brother is a friend forever.

He is so smart and so clever.

He will help you through thick and thin.

You'll be so glad that he's your kin.

He'll be your friend until the end.

So I thank God for giving me a special brother.

I love him so - can't you see,

because his branch completes our family tree.

Sisters are friends
who
share a special love.

My Sister, My Friend

Remember, Sis.

When we were growing up?

We laughed together.

We cried together.

We had our ups and downs.

But sisters are special people.

I just want you to know

that I can't imagine my life

without you in it.

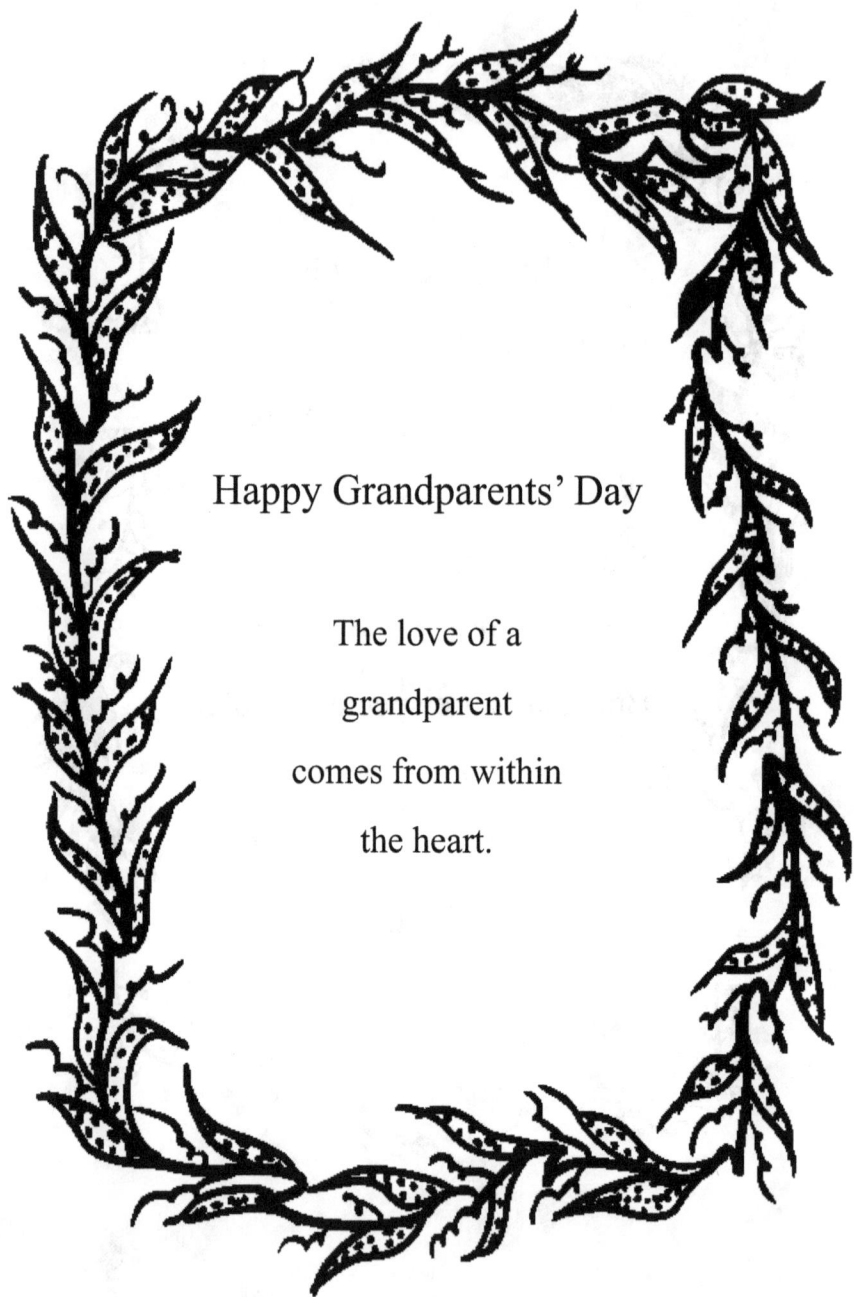

Happy Grandparents' Day

The love of a

grandparent

comes from within

the heart.

First Parents, Then Grandparents

No matter how old you are,

it's so hard to lose a Grandparent.

Remember Grandma

who use to kiss you when you hurt

your knee?

She used to bake those good cookies,

and take you shopping to buy all the

good stuff.

Remember Grandpa and all the

good stories he used to tell?

Love your grandparents

with all your heart.

Tomorrow, they may be gone.

You can grow
anything if you just
plant the seed.

God's Garden

God planted His garden,
And we were the flowers.
When He made rain,
We grew pretty and strong.
He gave us life that lasted
Just so long.
When a flower would die,
God gave it His grace,
And another one would take its
place.

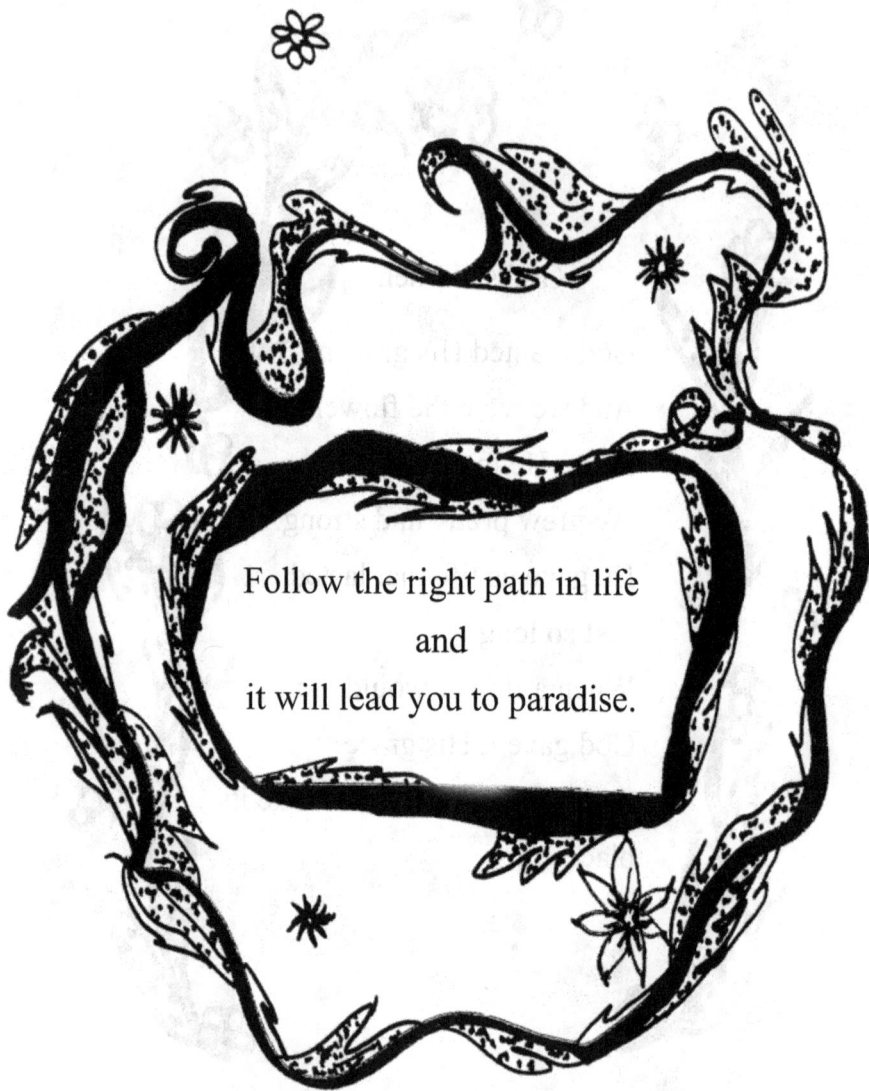

Follow the right path in life
and
it will lead you to paradise.

Heaven On My Mind

Dearest Lord, Heavenly Father,

If you have the time,

I have something on my mind.

I always wondered what heaven was like.

I pictured your gates painted a

beautiful white.

Is it true that you have no pain?

And is it true that you have no burdens?

I see the clouds so soft and calm,

just peaceful at rest.

I know now that my life was just a loan.

So I'll be thankful, Lord, until I see you at

this place called home.

*Life has a beginning
and
life has an end.*

God called my name,

and took away my pain.

Yes, I had a full life

and it's been blessed,

but God knew that I

needed a rest.

As time passes by, wipe your tears

and please don't cry.

I will miss my family and friends

and the laughter that we shared.

I ask God to bless all of you

and to keep you in His care.

So don't live in sorrow,

because tomorrow will be a bright, sunny day,

and I'll be with my Master.

    I'll be okay.

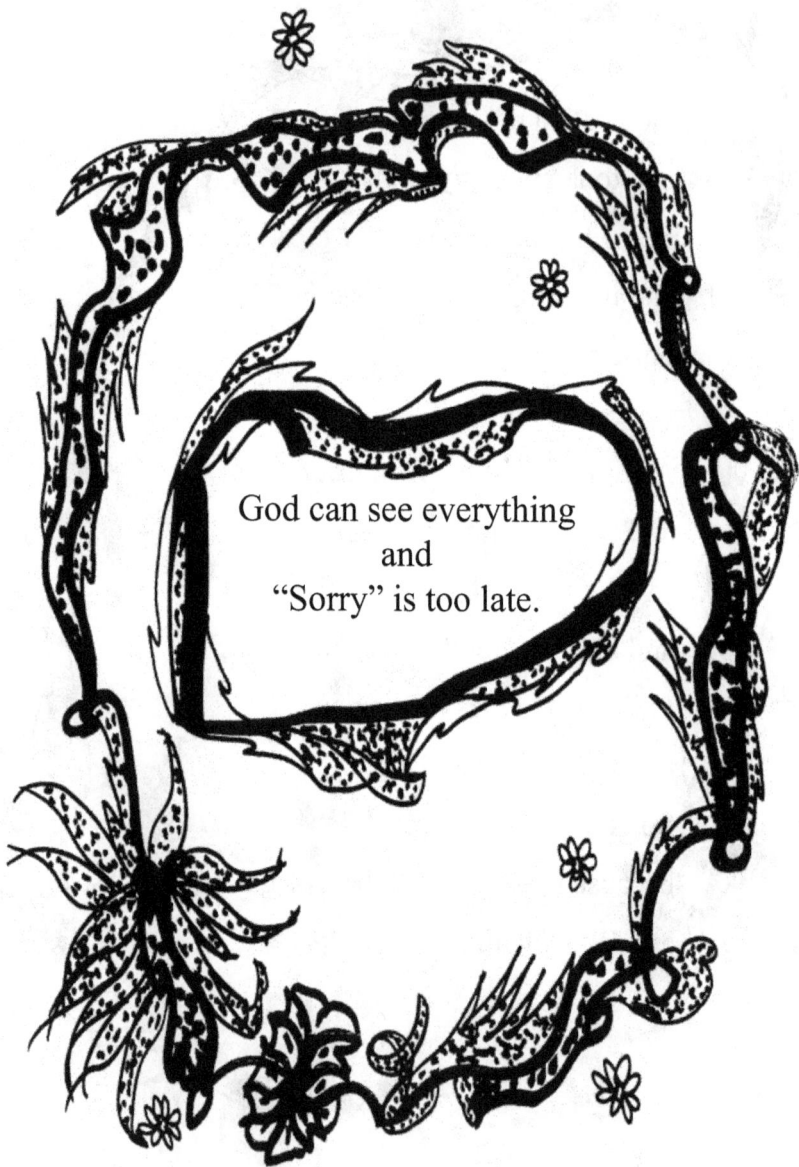

God can see everything
and
"Sorry" is too late.

To All My Creatures

I created all of you and gave you life.

I put you on this earth to live and to

show me your worth.

As I look down, I see all this awful mess,

I just can't believe my eyes.

I see all the money-hungry people stealing

large amounts from their own companies'

"How sad."

I see good people living a fine Christian life,

and I will bless them with paradise.

I gave all of you a good mind.

Will you please use?

Could you please think before you start to sin?

If you need help, just ask me.

Just remember,

it is I who put you on this earth, and it is I

who can take you away.

                              Your Savior,

                              God

God's Word

Dear Lord,

I just wonder what goes through your mind,

when you look down and see all this crime.

You know how some people live,

and yet you still can forgive.

Many people are living with pain and sorrow,

living each day not knowing,

what sadness will bring tomorrow.

I wonder if the killing and stealing will ever stop.

Lord, just hear our prayers,

for there's so much to pray for.

My Dear Child,

I want you to know,

that I really care,

and my thoughtful soul

I heard your prayers.

Just believe in Me and speak

to Me in prayers.

I will bless you for all your pain,

and give you faith in My Holy Name.

Don't ever take Me for granted,

because I made everyone

from a piece of clay,

and it is "I" who can take you away.

Just A Thought

One day as I was thinking of the future

and of the years that passed,

I looked out the window and stared at the grass.

When things got so bad I thought, Lord,

I know You're everywhere,

why then didn't You hear my prayers?

I thought of all the love and those

for whom I care, but mostly Lord,

the struggle in life and the pain of Jesus Christ.

We know our life is just a test,

and we're here to show You our best.

Sometimes, Lord, life gets a little troublesome

and we could use a rest.

Then I saw the brightness of a star and felt,

oh my God, You must have heard my thoughts,

and if You were to answer me,

maybe You would have said:

"Look, my child, how I've blessed you,

I put you on this earth

to show Me your worth.

You are breathing the air that I made,

and I protect you so you're not afraid.

And now, my child, if you think

you're at the end of your rope,

with very little hope,

just look around you,

there are others not so fortunate.

If you think you're not strong enough to make it,

and you don't care to see another rising of my sun,

Just Remember,

I Died For Everyone."

When we take
time for others,
God takes time
for us.

Thank God For Friends

If you help a friend in need,

God will bless you for a good deed.

Just lend a caring ear,

and a shoulder to catch the tears.

There's nothing you can say.

Just watch the blessings

that God sends your way.

Don't Be A Sinner

Try

To Be A Winner

One day I had a talk with God.

I said, "God, why is it that our world is so full

of pain?"

And God Said,

"Well, if all the sinners would look in the mirror,

they will see the blame."

And I asked God,

"Then why don't you help all the sinners?"

God said,

"Well, I help those who believe in me and pray.

As for all the sinners,

I only help those who try to help

themselves."

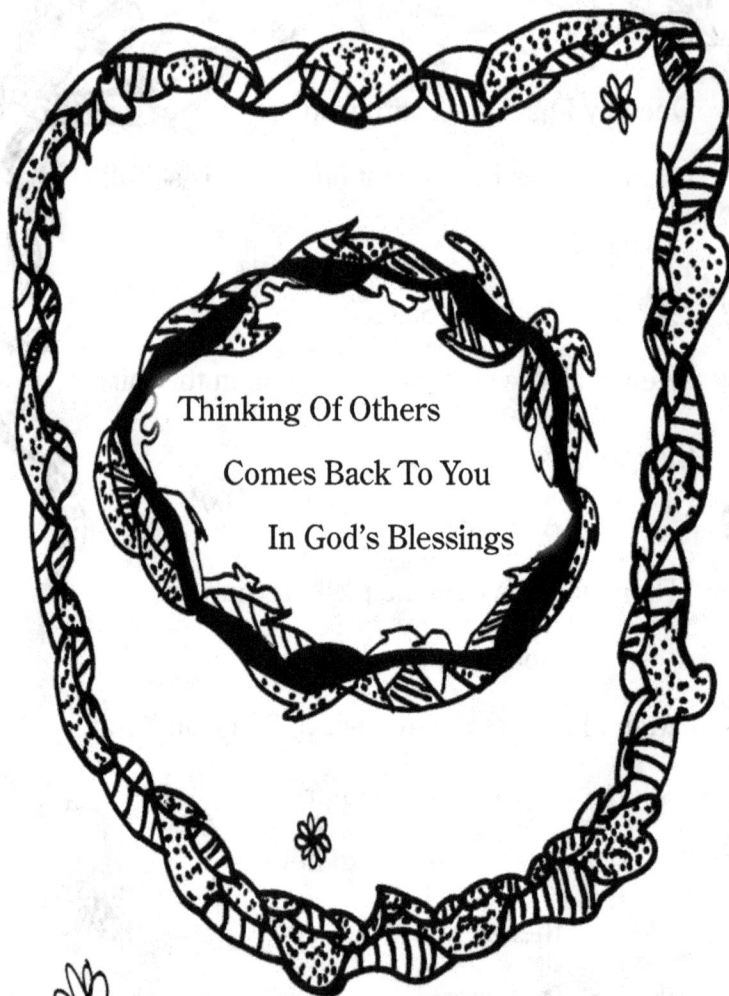

Thinking Of Others

Comes Back To You

In God's Blessings

Thinking of You

I lit a candle for you just yesterday

And hope God heard me as I began to pray.

I asked God to bless you and to keep you

in His glory, to always be near you in times of worry.

I asked God to give you courage

for the burdens you bear, to love you always,

and to keep you in His care.

When I think of you,

and the path that you have traveled,

only God knows what will be.

Maybe I'll get lucky

and someone will light a candle for me.

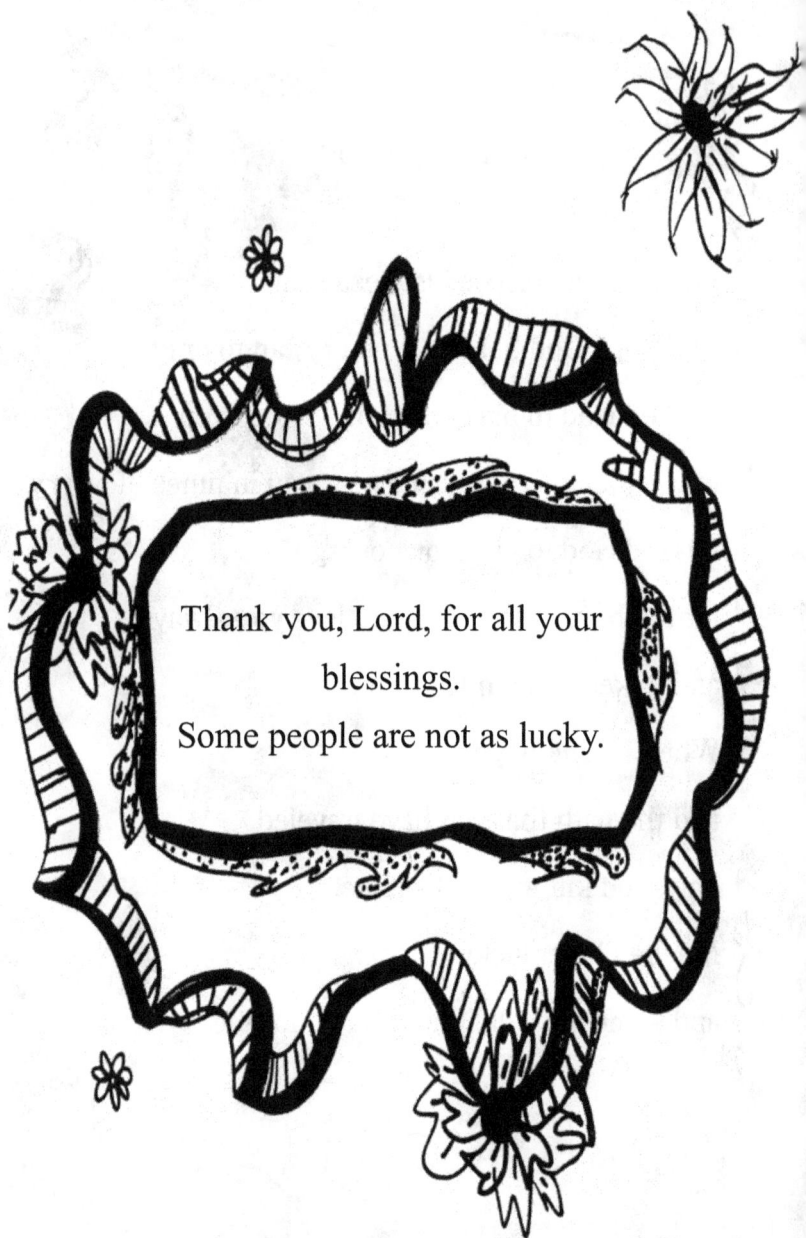

Thank you, Lord, for all your
blessings.
Some people are not as lucky.

Thanks Lord

Do you know Lord,

That you're always on my mind.

Somehow I don't think I thanked

you enough for being so kind.

You gave me good sight to see

right from wrong.

You were always there,

when I needed you the most.

You always answered my prayers.

You gave me hope to carry on.

I thank you Lord for being

my best friend.

After our tears are gone

God gives us His rainbow.

If I Were An Angel

If I were an angel,

I would protect you through the day.

I would ask God to take all your cares away.

I would always be there to wipe all your tears.

I would ask God to bless you,

through all of your years.

I would ask God to comfort you

in times of stress,

He knows that you did your best.

Always remember,

For every cloud

There is a beautiful rainbow

Just waiting for you.

That's My Business

I am a strong person, I can think for myself.

If I want to waste my money and yet put

no value on my life, that's my business.

I will listen to no one; if I want to do drugs,

that's my business.

I don't care if I crush the hearts of my family

and friends.

I will sneak around so my children don't follow

in my footsteps.

I don't care if my actions and my mood

get out of control.

I don't care if I bring sorrow and anquished feelngs

to my family and friends who try to help me,

because that's my business.

That's My Business

I don't care if I can't get along with others
and my bad habit is against the law.
I don't care if my best friend died from an
overdose, he/she didn't do it right,
but I know how.
I don't care if I don't have any friends.
I'm in control, that's their problem.
I have a mind of my own, and that's
my business.
I don't care about the look on Mom's face.
I know she's proud of me because
I have my life on the line.
I don't care about the tears running down
Mom and Dad's face as they lower me
into the ground,   BECAUSE
THAT WAS MY BUSINESS.

Time is like people.
They are both special.

A calendar is like your birthday,

on the last day you turn the page

and start another year.

You look back and remember all the

good memories.

Today on your special birthday,

I have the very best of all memories.

I get to share with you today

your birthday,

and I also have you for a very special

friend.

How Lucky

Can I Be

Lord, help me to help others.

A Nurse's Prayer

Lord, give me the strength to give

the best of my care,

to those in pain much for to be compared.

Let each passing of the day bring

a new reward as I make the right decisions,

I pray to the Lord.

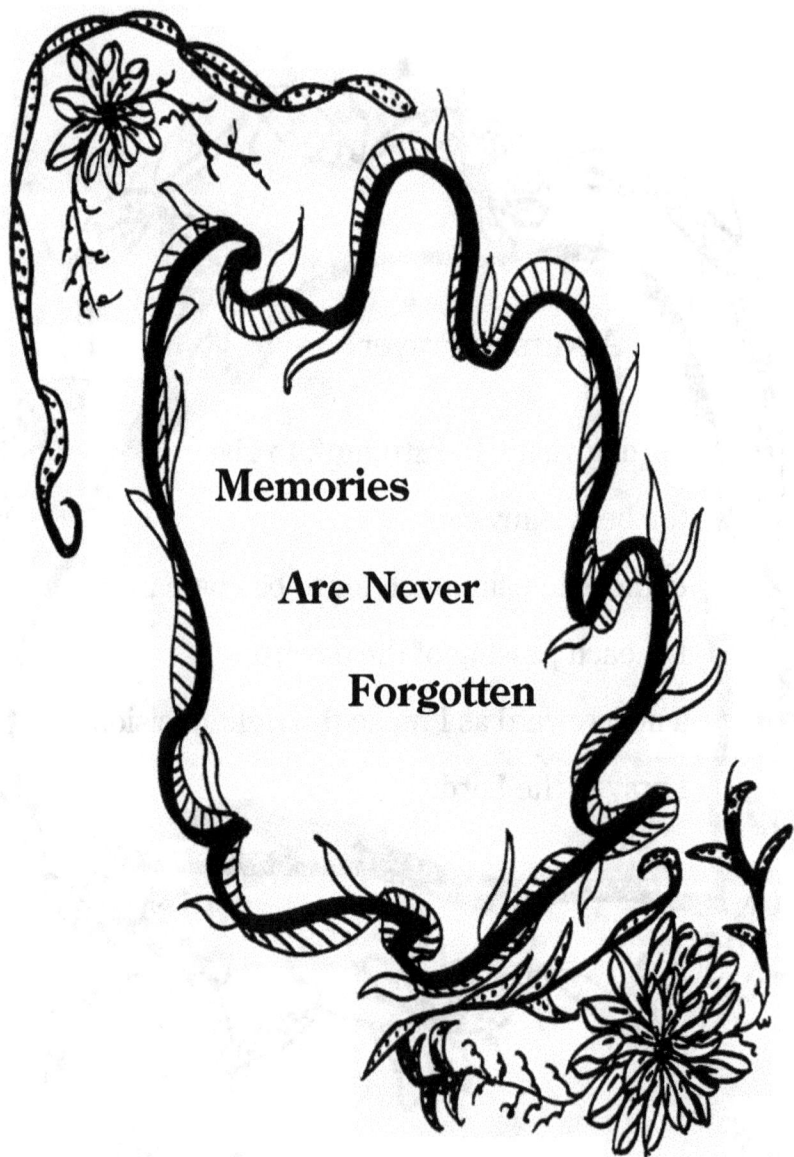

Memories

Are Never

Forgotten

I Still Remember

When I was small and just a little tot,

I still remember my dear Grandma,

and all the love I got.

My Grandma was a darn good cook,

I still remember sitting on her lap

while she read me a book.

I remember when she used to wipe

my little nose,

she would always say

       honey—just—blow.

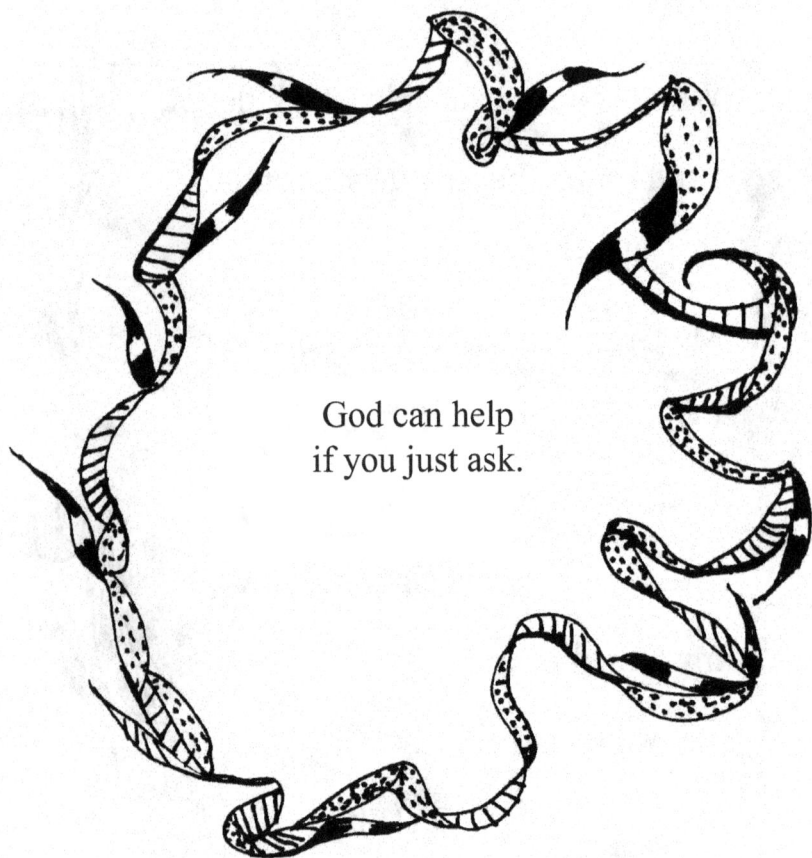

God can help
if you just ask.

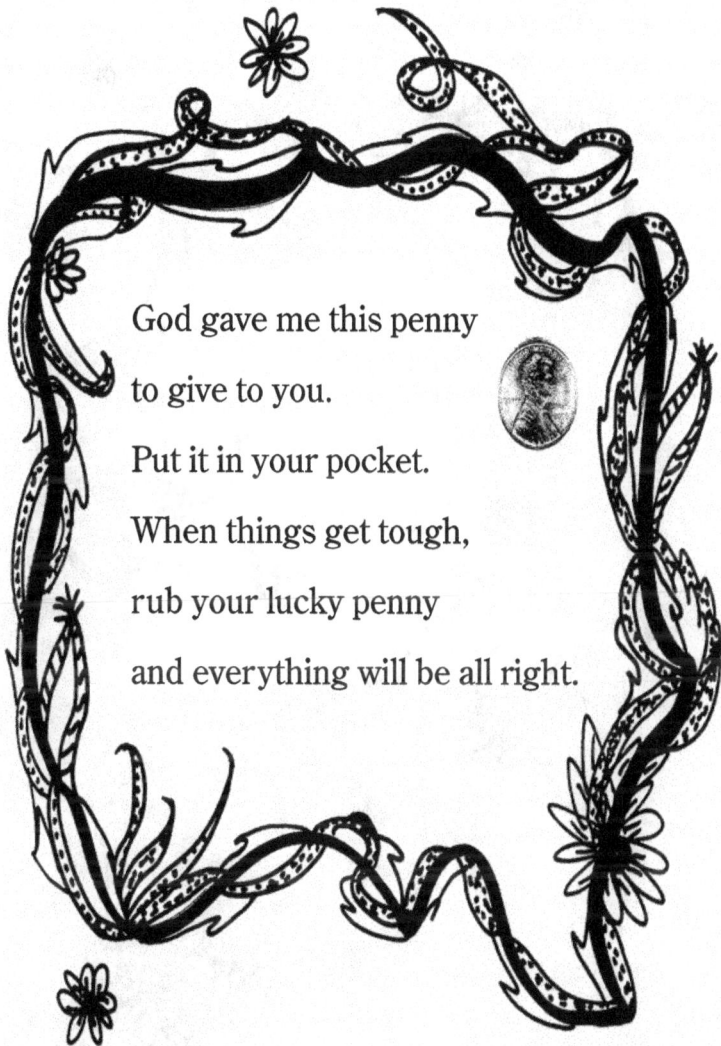

God gave me this penny

to give to you.

Put it in your pocket.

When things get tough,

rub your lucky penny

and everything will be all right.

Two Loving Hearts

That Are

Living Apart

We're Only Breaking Up On The Outside

We're only breaking up on the outside,

but we'll never break up on the inside.

These feelings we have for each other

we just can't hide.

As the years go by, the special love we had

will never die.

When I think of your smile,

I always feel happy inside for just a little while.

Yes, we're only breaking up on the outside,

but our hearts will never break up on the inside.

Lord, protect those

who protect us.

Lord, protect those

who protect us.

A Policeman's Prayer

Lord, as I start another day,

help me with patience I'll have to say.

Let me go with strength and a clear mind,

Lord help me if I should get into a bind.

Lord what's going to happen to the human race

if these criminals aren't put in their place?

Lord keep me safe as I try to fight crime,

stay by my side all of the time.

Thank You, Lord,
for all Your help.

We make a great team.

A Doctor's Prayer

Lord, as a doctor I do my best.

Some days are pleasant.

Some are a challenge

and some can be an awful test.

Please give me patience

And guide me through the day.

Stay by my side along the way.

Our prayers are always answered.

It just takes time.

Lord Where Were You Yesterday?

Lord where were you yesterday when my life
was falling apart?
I asked you Lord to comfort me
as I prayed with all my heart.
Somehow I felt so alone that the struggle
was mine to bear.
But Lord I know I wouldn't have made it
this far without all your love and care.

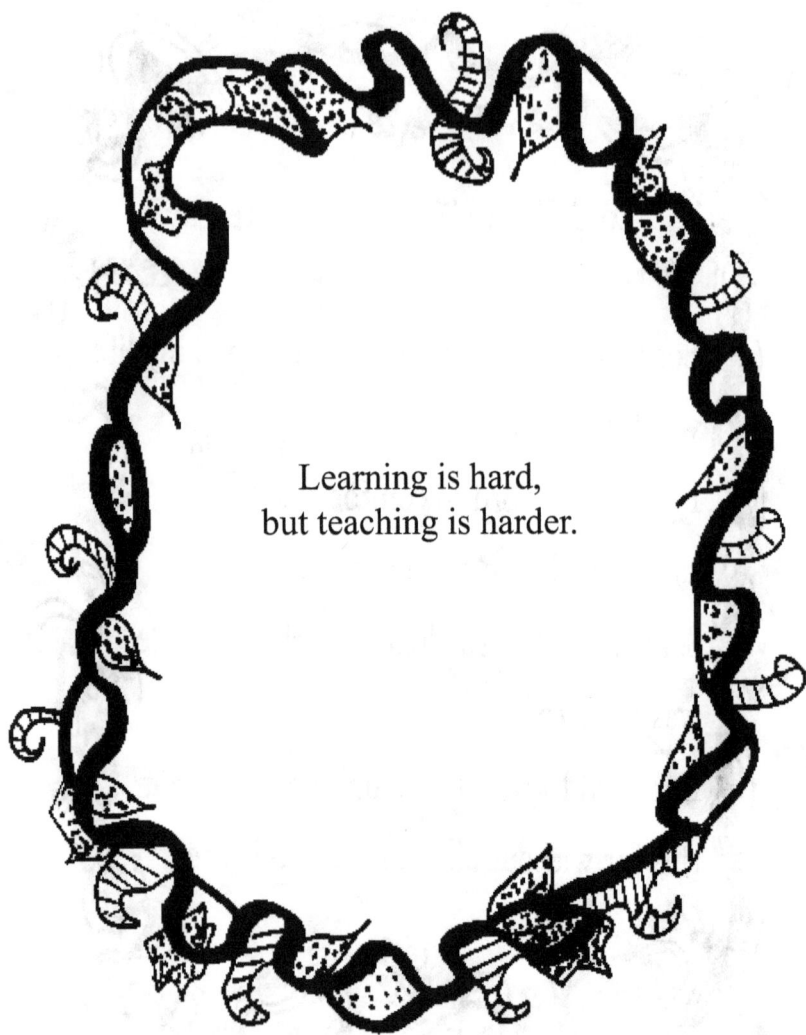

Learning is hard,
but teaching is harder.

A Teacher's Prayer

Lord as I sit at the front of the class,

I need your help with my daily task.

Lord, it's my job to teach these children

some knowledge, hopefully to prepare them

for college.

I do my best to teach them how to learn,

but they know that in my class good grades

they must earn.

God can change
your life
at any time.

God's Special Love

I met this man who had a warm hand.
He had a very special smile
And his laughter was funny.
Thank you, Lord, for making this man.
I'll try to make him happy the best I can.

Everyone loves to eat,
but no one likes to eat alone.
So thank God for all our
family and friends.

God set a special day aside for family and
Friends to get together;
For all those caring hearts to laugh, visit,
And to remember all the past memories;
To be thankful for all our blessings, and
For all our loved ones.

It's a time for sharing, giving, and
For turkey and pumpkin pie.
You know,
I bet that's why God called it
                    Thanksgiving.

The Final Word

Dearest Lord,

If you have a minute or two?

I'd like very much to talk to you.

The crime on earth is so out of control,

I wonder if these sinners even have a soul.

What goes through their mind,

when they are abusing or killing

innocent people for no reason.

Do they not think of the family and friends

they are leaving with broken hearts

and tears for the rest of their years.

You gave us a beautiful world to live in,

and some people just take it for granted.

Lord, if you can hear me?

Please help us and answer our prayers.

My Dearest Soul,

Just to ease your mind,

I want you to know that I heard every word.

I am also saddened at this awful mess.

I have given you a world to be proud of.

I gave you my ten commandments

to live by, and as I look down,

I see all these troubled things,

and I, too, could cry.

Thank you for the asking,

and I will bless you once again.

But my dear soul,

just keep praying and don't you worry.

Because Everybody Will Have Their Day

And

I Will Be The Judge

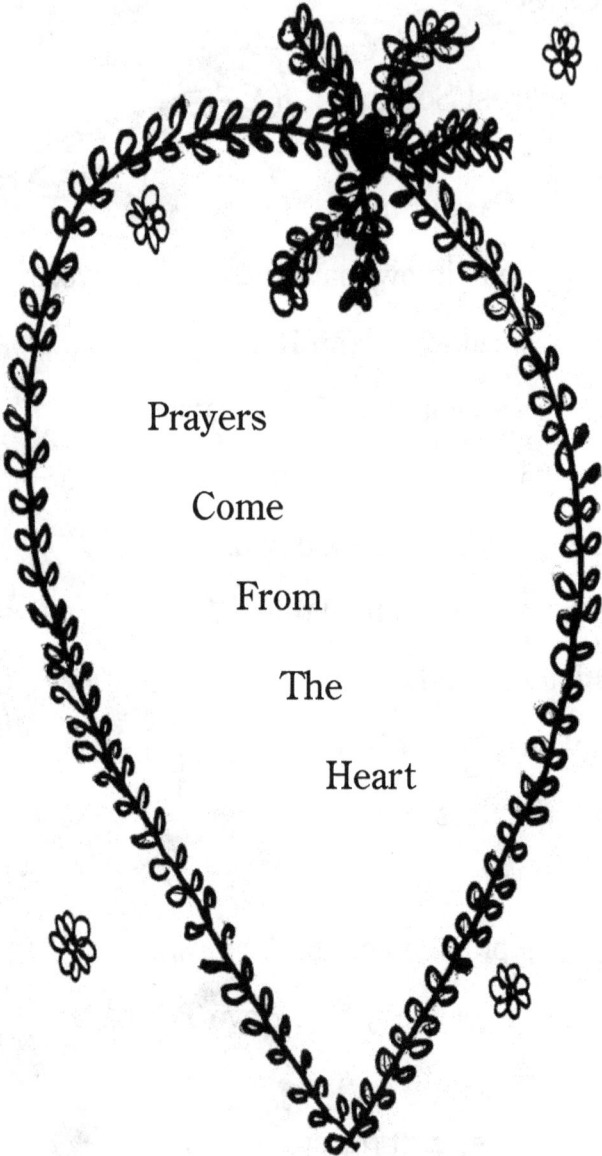

Prayers

Come

From

The

Heart

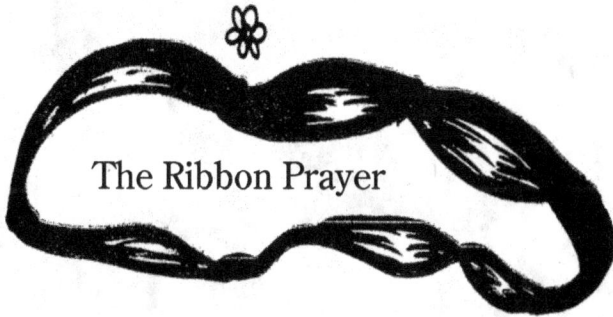

The Ribbon Prayer

Our Most Gracious Lord,

We hold this ribbon in our hands,

and pray that you bless us, we know you can.

Thank you Lord for all your blessings, and thank

you Lord for all your love.

We hold this ribbon in our hands,

and ask you Lord to bless us with peace on earth.

We hold this ribbon in our hands,

to thank you Lord from the bottom of our hearts.

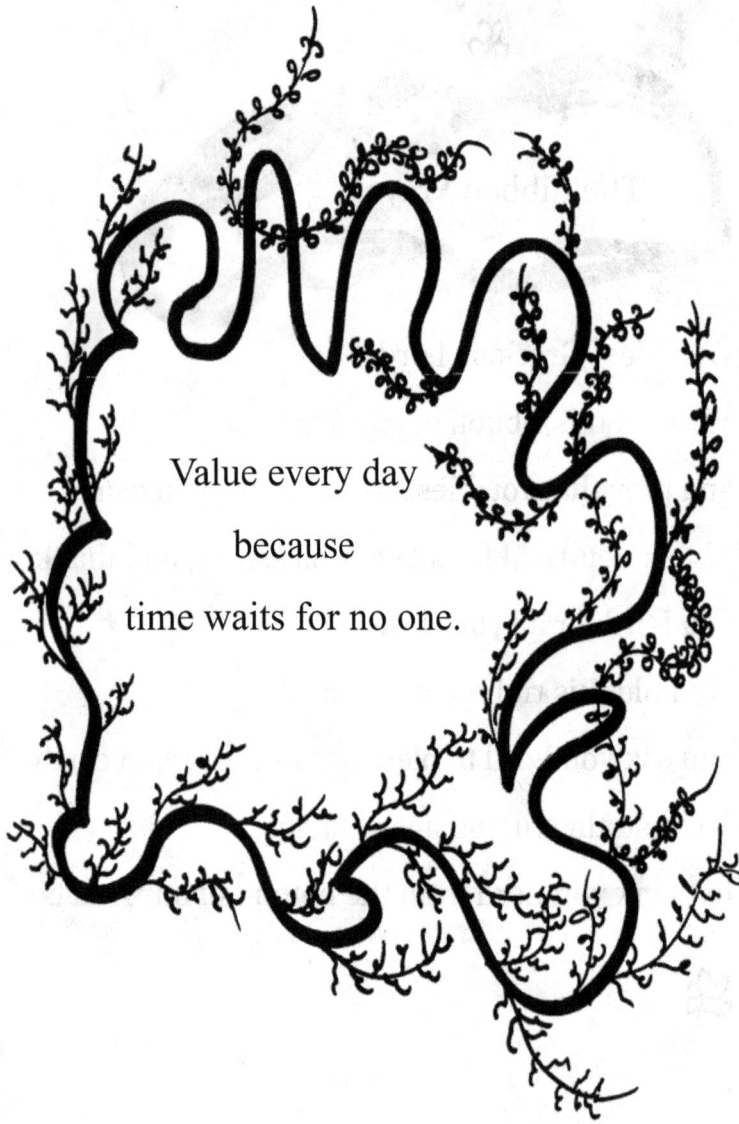

Value every day

because

time waits for no one.

Another Day Has Passed

Another day has passed.

It seemed to me it went so fast.

Knowing I would never get to live

that day again,

I worked so hard.

I hope I got everything in.

Answers From Heaven

If I should meet you God face to face,

there's so many unanswered questions about

the human race.

Why is it, God, there's so much suffering and pain?

At times it was such a struggle just to gain.

Why is there so much jealousy and hate?

Maybe we tried when it was too late.

Why is it God that so many people died

from cancer?

That alone to me was a mystery of an answer.

Nobody respects the treasures of others.

Some have stolen from their own sisters

and brothers.

I know we were rich in other ways

but God we need your help every passing

of the day.

My child, if I should answer you of all this
misfortune, you see this is my will that's
being done.

I alone am only to know the future, but I will
bless you for the asking and tell you this
in a simple way.

Remember my ten commandments?
I could have given you more but I only
gave you ten.

Now go back and read them from one to ten,
can't you see your answers for yourself?
This is why your life seemed so hard,
because this is what happens when you
don't go by the rules of the Lord.

Angels are there for you
when you need them the most.

The Blue Angels

Firemen are angels in blue suits.

They risk their lives to save others,

and their homes.

They are trained people and very special.

Whenever I hear a siren,

I think, there goes God's angels to help

someone in need.

Say a prayer and thank God

for all His special angels.

Don't ever take them for granted,

you may be the next one they save.

There is never
a
reason not to pray.

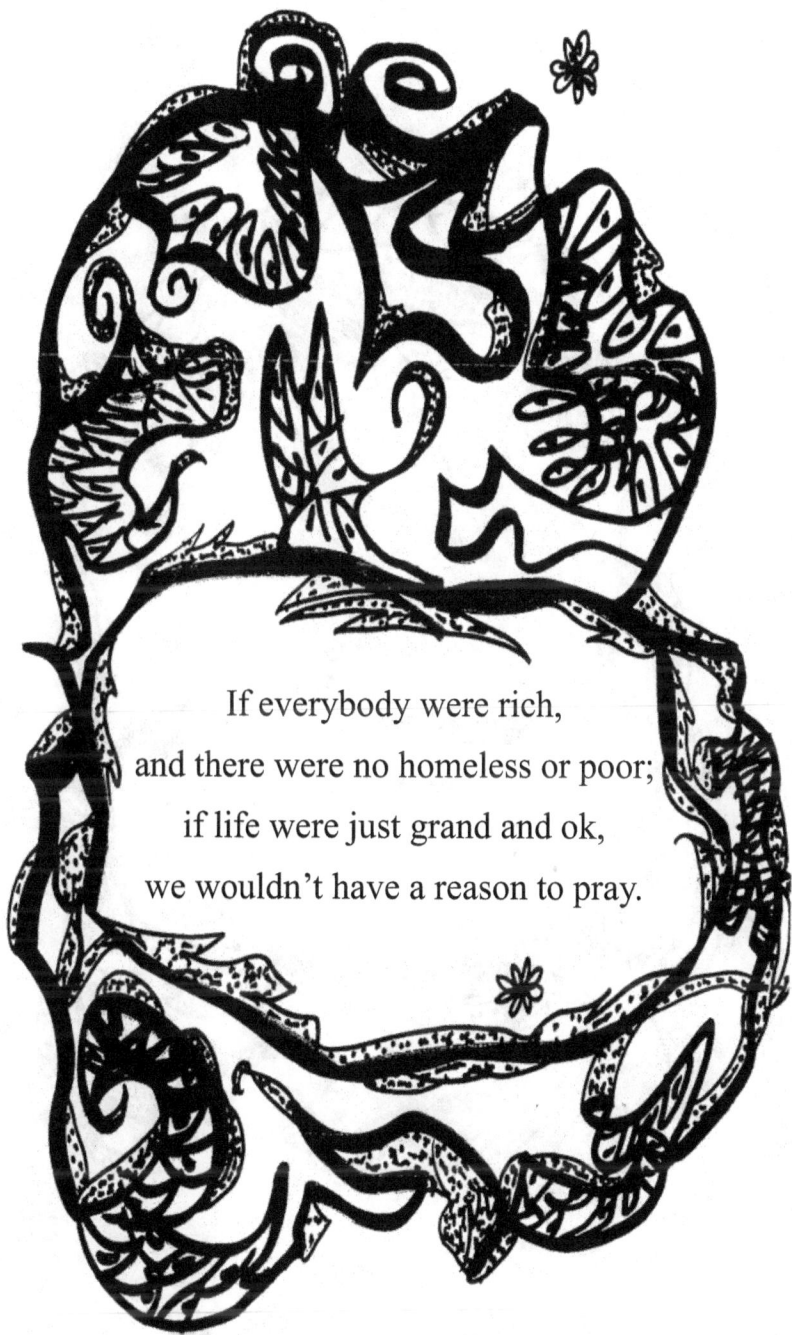

If everybody were rich,
and there were no homeless or poor;
if life were just grand and ok,
we wouldn't have a reason to pray.

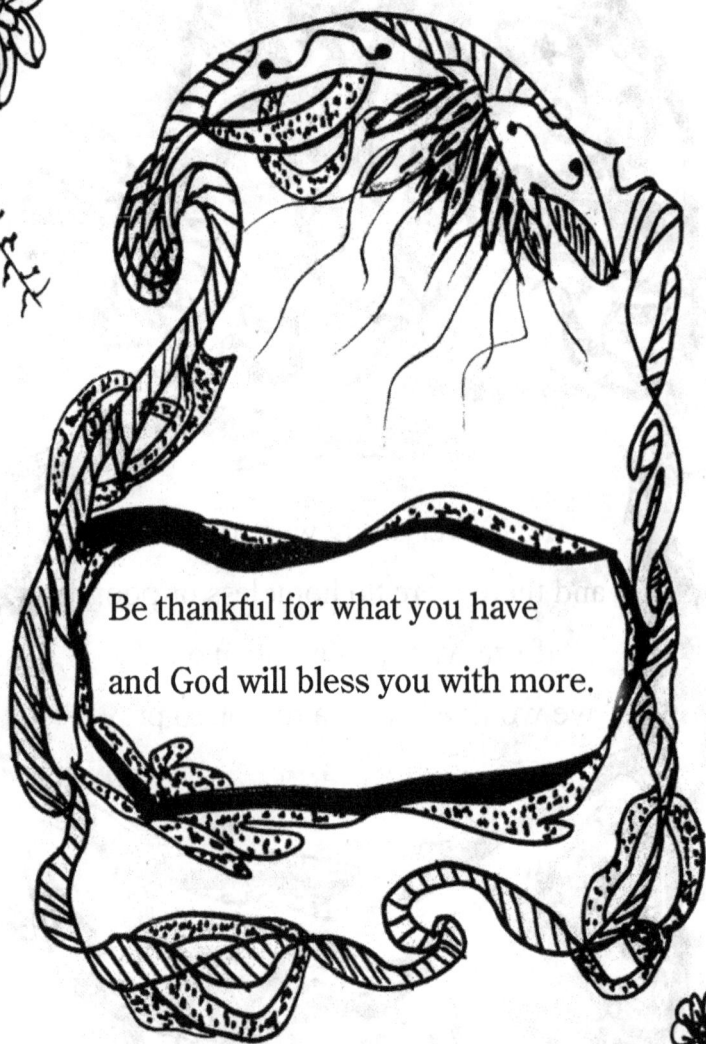

Be thankful for what you have

and God will bless you with more.

Miracles Of Love

I believe in miracles,

we see them every day.

Now I know God hears me when I pray.

God doesn't tell us where they are,

He knows we'll take them for granted.

God gives us His miracles in special

ways, and if you just look around,

His love is glowing every day.

So when you pray in times of trouble

or pain, God will hear you

and it will be your gain.

Our life is what we make it.

If you don't like it,

change it.

God Is Watching

God does everything for a reason.
We may not understand sometimes,
but you can bet it's for the good
of mankind.

You don't have to be in love with your
neighbors, but you don't have to burn down
their house or smash up their car neither.
What happened to "Peace On Earth",
and "Do Unto Others"?

Nobody wants to live in fear.
So say a prayer that God will hear.
God is our friend indeed,
and He made all of us from a tiny seed.
He didn't put us here to fight and tear
up His earth, but only to show Him
what we're worth.

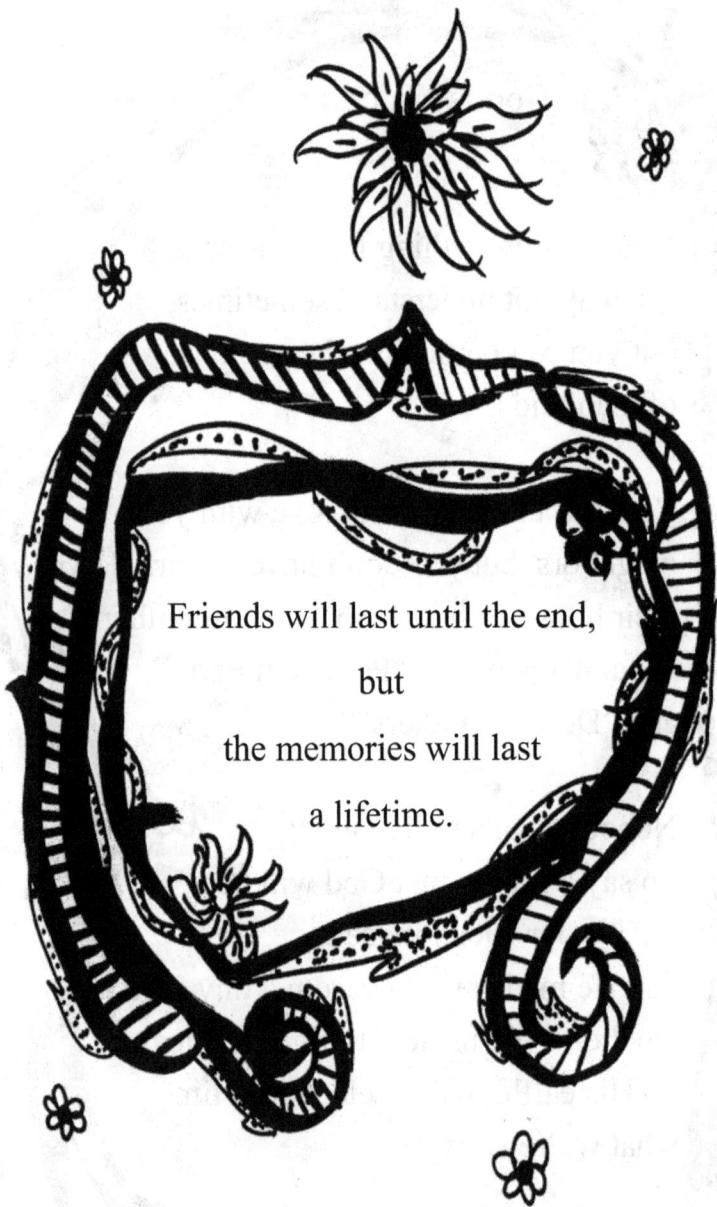

Friends will last until the end,

but

the memories will last

a lifetime.

A Lifetime Friend

Today I made a friend forever,

never thought it would happen to me

now or never.

God sent him to me I know,

because when I thank Him,

my heart just glows.

God put my love high on a beam you know

and looks down on me as my face gleams.

You can't buy my friend with money,

and for the rest of my life,

I'll call him honey.

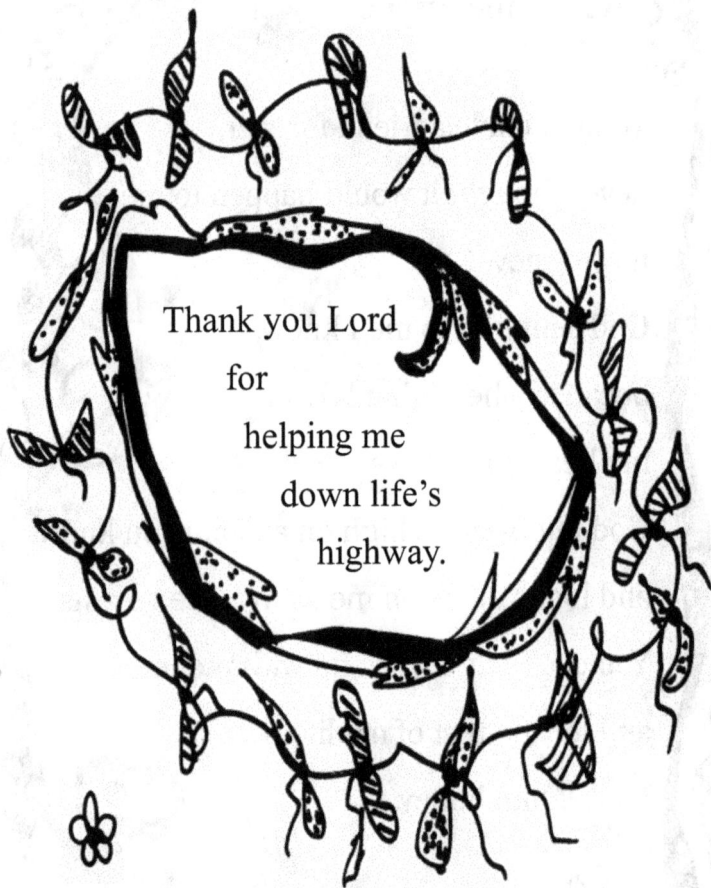

Thank you Lord
for
helping me
down life's
highway.

A Golden Year

Thank you Lord for letting me be 90.

I've lived a long life and been through a lot.

I thank you Lord for all that I got.

Yes Lord, I've had some ups and downs,

but somehow I still think I could paint

the town.

Thank you Lord for a year that was golden

and today I'm 90 and still holding.

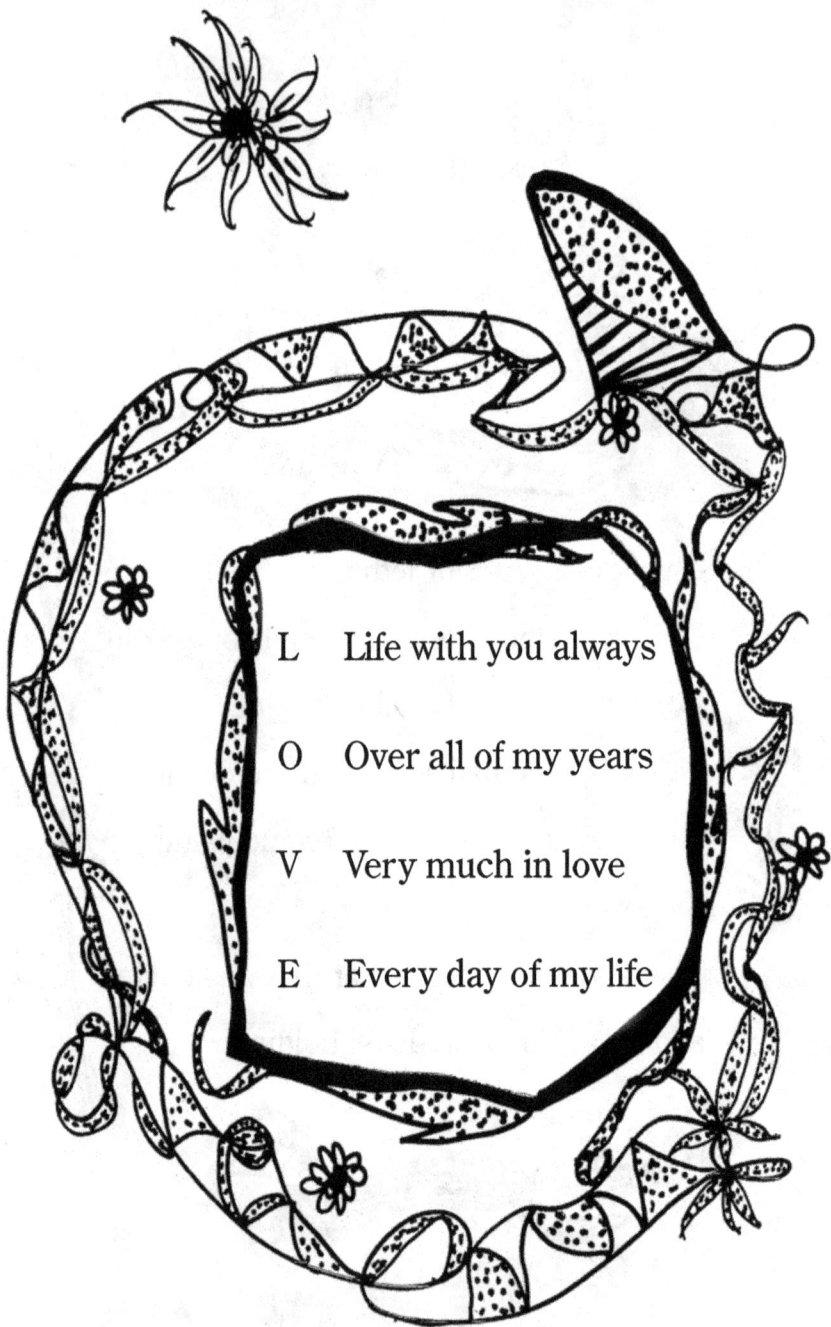

L   Life with you always

O   Over all of my years

V   Very much in love

E   Every day of my life

Love became a special thing,

the first day you put on your wedding ring.

As you treasure your band of gold,

your new memories will be locked

in your hearts to hold.

Life becomes more brighter, for now you

have a partner to care.

Happiness will be forever in all

that you both will share.

God will help you
when you're in pain.
He will bless you
in His Holy Name.

You know,
When you're down and blue,
God knows what you're going through.
So step aside and God will take you
On a magic ride.
Always trust and believe,
For God has a plan,
And you'll know it when
He takes your hand.

Share your troubles with God,

and

He will help you just for the asking.

Our King

God is our King,

and He protects us with His angels of wings.

He comforts us with His love

and keeps us warm.

Yes, we have so much to be thankful for.

So if we say a prayer each day of the month,

on December 31 we would have said 365 prayers,

and that's something to be proud of.

God is always there to
help if you just ask.

Help From God

God as I get out of bed

and start another day,

I ask you to go with me and help

me to keep my big mouth shut.

Please help me to be kind to others,

and to speak with respect.

Help me to do a good job

the best that I can.

Tomorrow I'll try to get through

the day without your helping hand.

If you never ask for help,
try walking alone.

Lord Walk With Me

Lord walk with me and I will follow.

Walk to the side of me, if you can,

and please hold my hand.

Lord talk with me and comfort my soul.

Life is a struggle just to reach my goal.

Help me with my burdens,

that fill my heart with pain.

Give me the strength to help myself,

and I'll try not to complain.

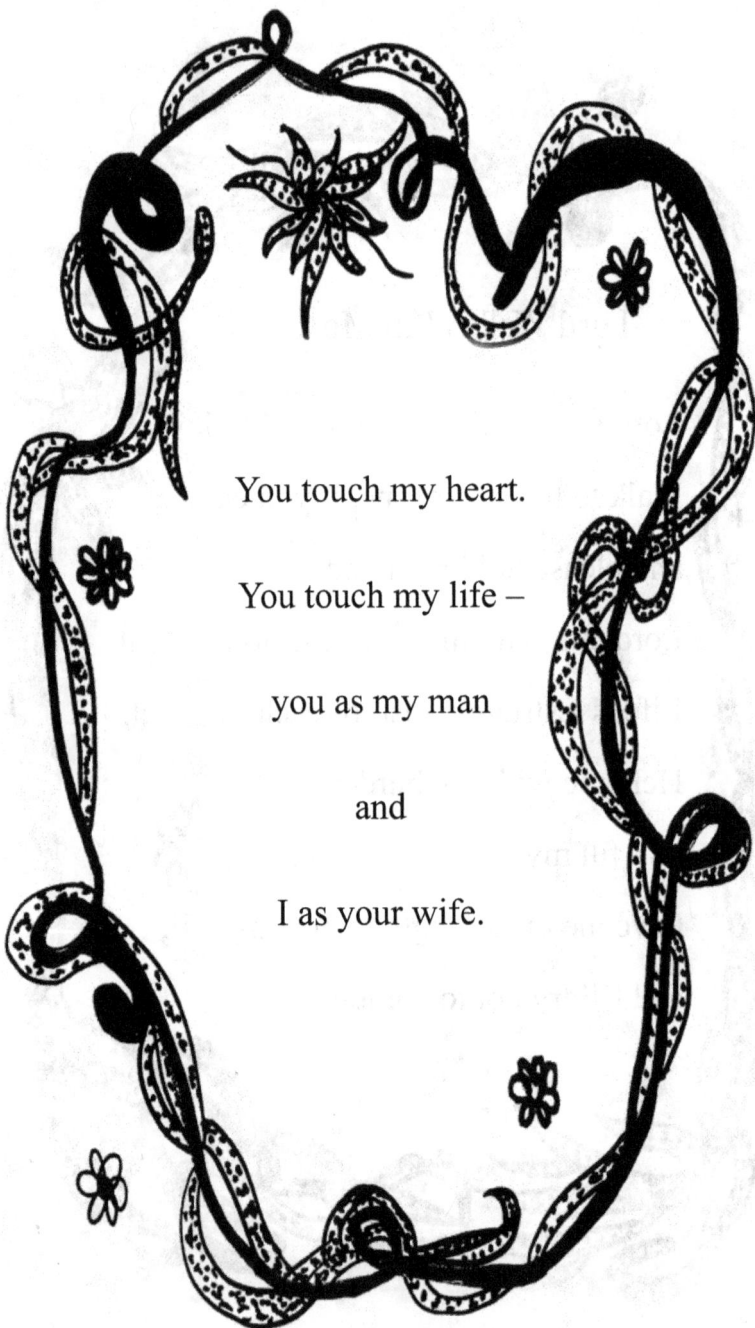

You touch my heart.

You touch my life –

you as my man

and

I as your wife.

Because of Love

Because of love I picked you.

I could have chosen from all the many,

but my heart wouldn't budge for any.

There was this special something about you.

I just couldn't explain.

I do know, that if I couldn't keep you that

I'd never be the same.

I'd always wonder where you were or maybe

how many burdens in life you would carry.

I'm so glad I played my cards just right,

because I'm the lucky one you picked to marry.

Old people have lived

for many years.

They have the memories

to prove it.

Old People Are Precious

Time has passed us by

for we've seen a lot through our eyes.

We remember raising our children,

and as they left the nest boy how we cried.

Life seemed like a struggle at times,

but God always helped us through.

As our youth slipped away and our pretty

hair turned grey there was nothing we could

do or say.

For we're not just old people.

If we took our pills we could still climb

the highest hill.

Even though some of us have never gone

to college, God has blessed us for too much

for now our lives are full of knowledge.

Don't make promises,

make plans.

Make it happen and

God will do the rest.

As each day goes by,

sometimes you feel that life is so hard

of a struggle you just want to die.

But no one ever reached their glory

just sitting around full of stress

and worry.

You have to climb to the top of life's ladder

and with hard work, when you reach the top,

nothing else will matter.

Hard work
never killed anyone,
but giving up
can be painful.

A Housewife's Prayer

Bless my house, oh Lord, I pray.

It's such a mess, I'll have to say.

With clothes, toys and clutter,

sometimes, Lord, I'm just tired

of being a mother.

Lord, I get so tired of doing dishes;

if only you could bless me with a few wishes.

I pray the Lord that someday you'll

send me a maid.

My friends think our house

Has been through a raid.

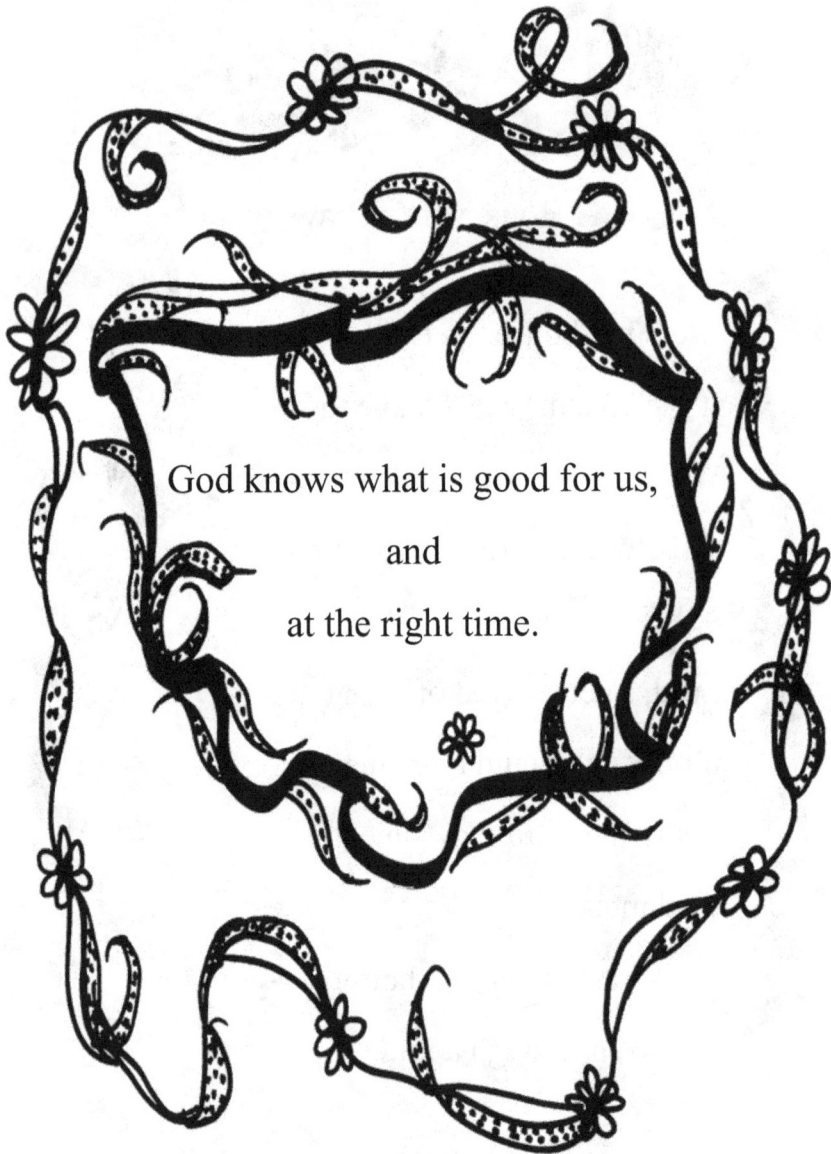

God knows what is good for us,

and

at the right time.

Blessings By The Hour

God is the light
and He is the glory.
Just ask Him for help
in time of worry.
Don't do it alone,
for He is near.
He is a good God,
for He is so dear.

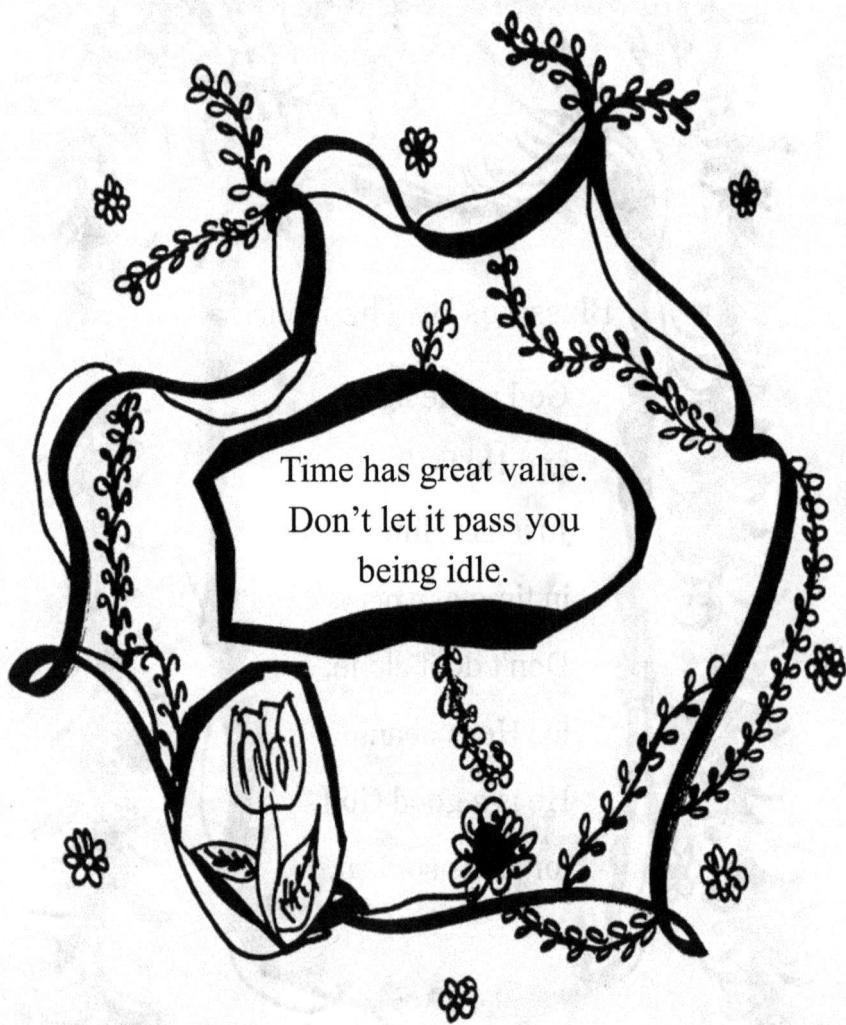

Time has great value.
Don't let it pass you
being idle.

Just For Today

Just for today, I'm going to live
this day to the fullest.
I'm going to think of myself and find
ways to improve myself.
Everybody on earth was born with
hidden talents.
It's up to us to seek them and use them
the best way we know how.
I will try to make every passing hour count,
so when I turn the page of this day,
it won't be blank.
When I meet you, God, at those golden gates,
I will be the one who can tell you of my
lifetime of happiness, and not the one who
stands before you in complete silence.

By reading this book, you have taken
your mind off your problems and
had a peaceful time for yourself.

Why?

You're worth it!
Everyone has some kind of pain they
have to deal with as life goes on:
the loss of a loved one,
a broken marriage,
an illness, or
fighting with drugs or alcohol.

Whatever is may be,
I hope God will bless you
and help you through it.

May God Give Us World Peace

And

Bring Our Loved Ones Together